The NORSEMEN

MYTHS *of the* WORLD

THE NORSEMEN

VIRGINIA SCHOMP

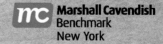
Marshall Cavendish
Benchmark
New York

⌒ For Rayce Joseph Romano ⌒

The author would like to thank Professor John Lindow, Department of Scandinavian Studies,
University of California, Berkeley, for his valuable comments
and careful reading of the manuscript.

Marshall Cavendish Benchmark 99 White Plains Road Tarrytown, New York 10591-9001
www.marshallcavendish.us Text copyright © 2008 by Marshall Cavendish Corporation Map copyright ©
2008 by Mike Regan. Illustration of the Nine Worlds on page 40 by Lisa Falkenstern. All rights reserved.
No part of this book may be reproduced or utilized in any form or by any means electronic or mechanical,
including photocopying, recording, or by any information storage and retrieval system, without permission
from the copyright holders. All Internet sites were available and accurate when this book was sent to press.
LIBRARY OF CONGRESS CATALOGING-IN-PUBLICATION DATA Schomp, Virginia. The Norsemen / by Virginia Schomp.
p. cm. — (Myths of the world) Summary: "A retelling of several key early Scandinavian myths, with back-
ground information describing the history, geography, belief system, and customs of the Norse World"—
Provided by publisher. Includes bibliographical references and index. ISBN 978-0-7614-2548-9
1. Mythology, Norse. I. Title. II. Series. BL860.S473 2007 398.209363—dc22 2007002772

EDITOR: Joyce Stanton ART DIRECTOR: Anahid Hamparian
PUBLISHER: Michelle Bisson SERIES DESIGNER: Michael Nelson

Images provided by Art Editor Rose Corbett Gordon and Alexandra Gordon from the following sources:
Cover: Fine Art Photographic Library/SuperStock Back cover: The Granger Collection, NY Page 1, 48, 50,
52, 64, 66, 67, 76, 82: Private Collection/Bridgeman Art Library; pages 2-3: Private Collection/The Maas
Gallery, London/Bridgeman Art Library; page 6: Arthur Thévenart/Corbis; page 7, 53, 84: Topham/The
Image Works; page 8: Bettmann/Corbis; pages 10-11, 32-33: Scala/Art Resource, NY; page 12, 24:
Nationalmuseum, Stockholm, Sweden/The Bridgeman Art Library; page 15: Bridgeman Art
Library/SuperStock; page 16, 69: Werner Forman/Corbis; page 18: Houses of Parliament, Westminster,
London/Bridgeman Art Library; page 19: Library of Congress, Washington D.C./Bridgeman Art Library;
page 20: Bass Museum of Art/Corbis; page 22: Private Collection/Lauros/Giraudon/Bridgeman Art Library;
page 26: Private Collection/Photo © Bonhams, London/Bridgeman Art Library; page 27: Blommér, Nils
Johan: Freja Seeking her Husband, The National Museum of Fine Arts, Stockholm; page 28, 42, 44, 72, 74:
The Granger Collection, NY; page 30, 63: Werner Forman/TopFoto/The Image Works; page 34, 36: Réunion
des Musées Nationaux/Art Resource, NY; page 39, 45, 56, 61, 85: Mary Evans Picture Library/The Image
Works; page 47: Ole Haupt, Ny Carlsberg Glyptotek, Copenhagen; page 55: Arni Magnusson Institute,
Reykjavik, Iceland/Bridgeman Art Library; page 57: Royal Library, Copenhagen, Denmark/Bridgeman Art
Library; page 58, 60: Charles Walker/Topfoto/The Image Works; page 70, 88: Werner Forman/Art Resource,
NY; page 78, 80: Yale Center for British Art, Paul Mellon Collection/Bridgeman Art Library; page 81: Ted
Spiegel/Corbis; page 87: Bibliotheque des Arts Decoratifs, Paris/Archives Charmet/Bridgeman Art Library;
page 90: The Art Archive/Bodleian Library Oxford.

Printed in Malaysia
135642

Front cover: The Valkyries carry fallen heroes to the paradise of Valhalla.
Half-title page: A giant eagle kidnaps Idun, the goddess of eternal youth.
Title page: The thunder god Thor could make the Earth shake with a blow from his magic hammer.
Back cover: One-eyed Odin was the king of the gods.

CONTENTS

THE MAGIC *of* MYTHS

EVERY ANCIENT CULTURE HAD ITS MYTHS. These timeless tales of gods and heroes give us a window into the beliefs, values, and practices of people who lived long ago. They can make us think about the BIG QUESTIONS that have confronted humankind down through the ages: questions about human nature, the meaning of life, and what happens after death. On top of all that, myths are simply great stories that are lots of fun to read.

What makes a story a myth? Unlike a narrative written by a particular author, a myth is a traditional story that has been handed down from generation to generation, first orally and later in written form. Nearly all myths tell the deeds of gods, goddesses, and other divine beings. These age-old tales were once widely accepted as true and sacred. Their primary purpose was to explain the mysteries of life and the origins of a society's customs, institutions, and religious rituals.

Above:
The Valkyries were warrior maidens of Odin, king of the gods.

It is sometimes hard to tell the difference between a myth and a heroic legend. Both myths and legends are traditional stories that may include extraordinary elements such as gods, spirits, magic, and monsters. Both may be partly based on real events in the distant past. However, the main characters in legends are usually mortals rather than divine beings. Another key difference is that legends are basically exciting action stories, while myths almost always express deeper meanings or truths.

Mythology (the whole collection of myths belonging to a society) played an important role in ancient cultures. In very early times, people created myths to explain the awe-inspiring, uncontrollable forces of nature, such as thunder, lightning, darkness, drought, and death. Even after science began to develop more rational explanations for these mysteries, myths continued to provide comforting answers to the many questions that could never be fully resolved. People of nearly all cultures have asked the same basic questions about the world around them. That is why myths from different times and places can be surprisingly similar. For example, the people of nearly every ancient culture told stories about the creation of the world, the origins of gods and humans, the cycles of nature, and the afterlife.

Tyr, the bravest of the Norse war gods, battles the terrible wolf Fenrir.

Thor, god of thunder and lightning, drove a noisy chariot pulled by two gigantic goats.

Mythology served ancient cultures as instruction, inspiration, and entertainment. Traditional tales offered a way for the people of a society to express their fundamental beliefs and values and pass them down to future generations. The tales helped preserve memories of a civilization's past glories and held up examples of ideal human qualities and conduct. Finally, these imaginative stories provided enjoyment to countless listeners and readers in ancient times, just as they do today.

The MYTHS OF THE WORLD series explores the mythology of some of history's greatest civilizations. Each book opens with a brief look at the culture that created the myths, including its geographical setting, political history, government, society, and religious beliefs. Next comes the fun part: the stories themselves. We based our retellings of the myths on a variety of traditional sources. The new versions are fun and easy to read. At the same time, we have strived to remain true to the spirit of the ancient tales, preserving their magic, their mystery, and the special ways of speech and avenues of thought that made each culture unique.

As you read the myths, you will come across sidebars, or text boxes, highlighting topics related to each story's characters or themes. The sidebars in *The Norsemen* include quoted passages from early tales, poems, and other original Scandinavian works. The sources for these quotations are noted on page 94. You will find lots of other useful information at the back of the book as well, including a glossary of difficult terms, a biographical dictionary of Norse writers, examples of the modern-day legacy of the myths, suggestions for further reading, and more. Finally, the stories are illustrated with both ancient and modern paintings, sculptures, and other works of art inspired by mythology. These images can help us better understand the spirit of the myths and the way a society's traditional tales have influenced other cultures through the ages.

Now it is time to begin our adventures with the Norsemen. We hope that you will enjoy this journey to a land of fire and ice, mighty gods and cunning dwarfs, evil giants and menacing monsters. Most of all, we hope that the sampling of stories and art in this book will inspire you to further explorations of the magical world of mythology.

Part 1
MEET *the* NORSEMEN

The NORSE WORLD

THE NORSEMEN WERE THE ANCIENT PEOPLE OF Scandinavia, the area of northern Europe that includes present-day Norway, Sweden, Denmark, and Iceland. They lived in a world that was harsh and forbidding. The winters in Scandinavia are fierce, with just a few hours of daylight between long cold nights. The summers are warm but brief. The landscape is rugged, with huge mountain ranges, grand lakes and rivers, and high cliffs overlooking the crashing waves of the North Atlantic and Arctic Oceans and the Baltic Sea.

The men and women who settled in these inhospitable lands had to be tough. They spent their lives struggling against the cold and dark, cruel storms and howling winds, hungry wolves and fierce neighboring tribes. In a world where almost everything seemed to be against them, the Norsemen came to value courage above all other qualities. They believed that there was no greater glory than to die fearlessly battling the world's evils. They honored men and women who faced life's hardships

Opposite:
The brave and beautiful Valkyries charged down to Earth on their flying horses.

Previous page:
Norse raiders approach a quiet settlement in their swift wooden longships.

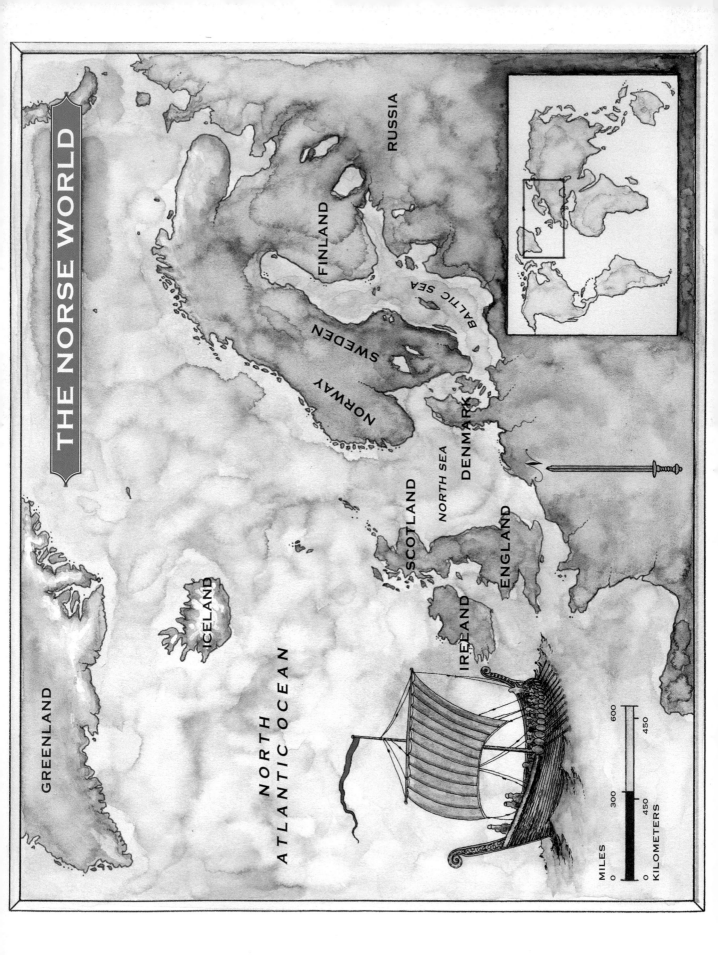

THE NORSE WORLD

GREENLAND

ICELAND

NORTH
ATLANTIC OCEAN

NORWAY

SWEDEN

FINLAND

RUSSIA

BALTIC SEA

DENMARK

SCOTLAND

NORTH SEA

ENGLAND

IRELAND

MILES
0   300   600

KILOMETERS
0   450   450

without bitterness, with a sense of humor and a spirit of adventure. They were intensely loyal to their kinfolk and leaders but also prided themselves on their self-reliance. In battle a Norse warrior might ignore his leader's commands and charge into danger if he saw a chance to avenge a friend's death or achieve lasting fame through daring deeds.

The stories told by these hardy adventurers reflected their harsh environment and heroic outlook on life. One of the main themes of Norse mythology is the endless struggle of the gods against the forces of cold, darkness, and evil. The Norse gods are colorful individuals who pursue exciting adventures in a world of storm-tossed oceans and ice-bound mountain caves. Although they have superhuman powers, even the gods are fated to die. Doom awaits them at Ragnarok, the final battle that will bring about the destruction of the world. Despite their knowledge of their fate, the gods face life like the Norsemen themselves, with unflinching courage, a lively wit, and robust joy.

Many adventurous Norsemen braved stormy seas in pursuit of fame and fortune.

RAIDERS, TRADERS, *and* EXPLORERS

THE HISTORY OF THE NORSEMEN SPANNED NEARLY three thousand years. It began with a group of related tribes known as the Germanic peoples. It ended with the most famous Norsemen of all, the Vikings.

Historians have traced the roots of Norse culture all the way back to the Scandinavian Bronze Age, which began around 1600 BCE. During the Bronze Age, southern Scandinavia was home to several Germanic tribes. The Germanic peoples were skilled shipbuilders, navigators, and craftworkers. They had no written language, but they left behind spectacular rock carvings and metal figures of gods and goddesses. These ancient artifacts are the earliest evidence of a rich mythological world populated with hundreds of divine beings.

From about the third to the sixth century CE, many of the Germanic tribes moved across central and western Europe in a series of wars and migrations. During this Migration Age, Germanic peoples settled in

Opposite: Early Scandinavians left behind fascinating pictures in stone. These figures may be warriors showing off their fighting skills.

The British fight off a Viking invasion in 878 CE.

Britain, France, Spain, Italy, and as far south as northern Africa. Wherever they went, they brought along their ancient beliefs and their tales of heroic kings, mighty gods, and evil giants.

By the end of the eighth century, most parts of Europe had converted to Christianity. In Scandinavia, however, the ancient Norse world of gods and giants endured. A patchwork of small kingdoms emerged, each ruled by a rich and powerful chieftain. To expand their kingdoms, chieftains sometimes led small bands of loyal followers into battle against neighboring territories. Some chieftains also raided foreign lands. Traveling in swift longships, the Scandinavian warrior bands staged hit-and-run attacks on monasteries and seaports in Britain and along the western European coast. The people who lived in terror of the fierce invaders gave them a variety of names, including Northmen or Norsemen. The Scandinavians called their warriors Vikings, from the Old Norse word *víkingr,* meaning "raider" or "pirate."

For more than two centuries, the Vikings built fame and fortune through their raids. Some warriors settled in the lands they had plundered, carving out colonies that stretched over large areas of western Europe. Viking raiders and traders also ventured east, establishing settlements in what is now Russia. Viking explorers even crossed the uncharted waters of the North Atlantic Ocean in search of new lands.

They built large settlements in Iceland and smaller colonies amid the snow and ice of Greenland. Around the year 1000, the Viking explorer Leif Eriksson sailed west from Greenland and became the first European to set foot in North America.

In time large areas of Scandinavia united under a single strong ruler, and the three kingdoms of Denmark, Norway, and Sweden began to emerge. Christianity took hold in these kingdoms, uprooting old beliefs and customs. Raiding and trading expeditions gave way to less perilous pursuits, such as farming, business, and government. Other powers overshadowed Scandinavian influence in western Europe. By the end of the eleventh century, the Viking Age had faded away.

Viking explorers led by Leif Eriksson reached North America nearly five hundred years before Columbus.

A variety of systems of dating have been used by different cultures throughout history. Many historians now prefer to use BCE (Before Common Era) and CE (Common Era) instead of BC (Before Christ) and AD (Anno Domini), out of respect for the diversity of the world's peoples.

SCANDINAVIAN SOCIETY

THE SOCIETY OF THE NORSEMEN WAS DIVIDED INTO three classes: nobles, freemen, and thralls. The noble class included chieftains and warriors with a variety of ranks and titles. Their wealth and power came from their control of land and men. The highest-ranking nobles were the jarls, or earls. These powerful men owned vast estates and commanded large bands of loyal warriors who pledged to follow them on raids and other expeditions.

The majority of Scandinavians belonged to the freemen class. This large group consisted of farmers and all other free working people. Farm families typically included not only a couple and their children but also the farmer's parents, unmarried brothers and sisters, and other relatives. All of the members of this large extended family lived together in a long rectangular dwelling called a longhouse. Once or twice a year, the men of the household took part in the Things, democratic assemblies where issues concerning the community were

Opposite: Norse women are thought to have been brave and outspoken, like the Valkyries of Norse mythology.

Early Scandinavian farmers raised reindeer for their milk, meat, and hides.

decided. Freemen also might venture away from home to trade or to join raiding expeditions.

Thralls, or slaves, made up the lowest class in Scandinavian society. Most thralls were foreigners who had been captured in raids and warfare. They had few rights or privileges. Slaves worked mainly as manual laborers or household servants, performing the hardest and dirtiest chores. However, slaves with special skills or beauty sometimes enjoyed a respected position in the household, perhaps serving as the manager of an estate or governess to their owners' children.

Women belonged to the same class as their fathers or husbands. Although Scandinavian society was dominated by men, women had important rights under the law. For example, wives had the right to own and inherit their own property and to divorce their husbands. Women also enjoyed considerable respect, responsibility, and influence within their homes. The brave and outspoken women of Norse mythology reflected this real-world status. Among the most famous Norse mythological females were the Valkyries, warrior maidens who were believed to lead the souls of fallen heroes to the paradise known as Valhalla.

GODS *of* WAR, GODS OF PLENTY

THE MAIN GROUP OF NORSE GODS WERE THE POWERFUL, warlike Aesir. Their king was Odin, god of war and wisdom. Odin's wife was Frigg, who could foresee the future. His oldest son was Thor, whose mighty hammer struck terror in the hearts of his enemies. Other leading Aesir included Tyr, the bravest of the war gods, and Balder, god of light, joy, and beauty. All of the Aesir lived together in the magnificent halls of Asgard, a realm far above the world of humans.

A second group of gods, the Vanir, were associated with fertility. The Norsemen believed that the Vanir were responsible for bountiful harvests, good fishing, and healthy children. Three of these ancient gods lived with the Aesir in Asgard: Njord, god of the sea; Frey, god of the harvest; and Freyja, goddess of love and fertility.

In addition to the gods and goddesses, a host of other supernatural beings filled the mythological world. Beautiful light elves roamed the lakes and forests, while dark elves dwelt underground. Dwarfs

Opposite: Thor's mighty hammer was the gods' best defense against the menacing giants.

The gods and goddesses peer down into the world of humans.

mined for treasure in deep caverns and crafted magical objects for the gods. Menacing giants lurked in fire, storm clouds, and the mountains. Among the most fearsome of all giants were the evil frost giants, who sent icy winds and deadly avalanches down from the frozen mountaintops. The frost giants were the natural enemies of both gods and humans. In time their undying hatred would bring about the death of the gods and the end of the world in the final battle of Ragnarok.

FAMILY TREE *of the* NORSE GODS

The two main groups of Norse deities were the Aesir and Vanir. The Aesir were associated with war and destiny, while the Vanir were gods of fertility. The most important gods and goddesses from each group are listed below.

AESIR

ODIN ···· **FRIGG**

ODIN
King of the gods; god of war, wisdom, learning, and magic

FRIGG
Wife of Odin and queen of the Aesir; goddess of marriage and motherhood

THOR
God of thunder, lightning, weather, and crops

HEIMDALL
Guardian of the bridge Bifrost

TYR
God of war and justice

BALDER
God of light, joy, purity, innocence, and beauty

HOD
Blind god of darkness

VANIR

NJORD
God of the sea

FREY
God of sunshine, rain, peace, prosperity, and the harvest

FREYJA
Goddess of love, fertility, and magic

IDUN
Goddess of fertility, youth, and the spring

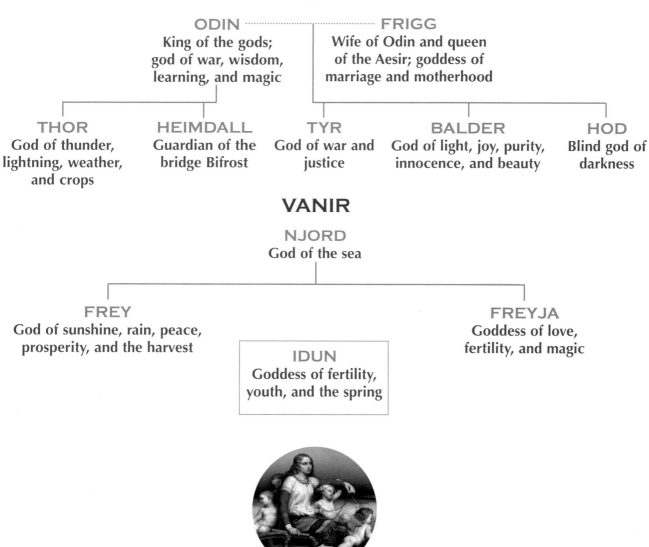
Freyja

KEEPING *the* FAITH

*T*HE NORSE RELIGION HAD NO CENTRAL CHURCH AND no creed, or specific set of religious beliefs. As a result the Scandinavians' ideas about their gods varied from person to person and place to place. However, all Norsemen shared a common heritage, which included many traditional beliefs and practices as well as their ancient body of myths.

During the Viking Age, the Scandinavians built temples to honor their gods. For most of their history, though, the Norsemen worshipped in sacred groves, forests, and other open spaces. A chieftain or other respected leader led the community in observing public rituals, feasts, and festivals honoring the gods. One of the most important ways to secure a god's blessings was through offerings of food; valuable objects such as tools, jewelry, and weapons; and sacrificial animals. Archaeologists exploring ancient Scandinavian offering sites have also

Opposite: This illustration of Odin comes from a collection of ancient Scandinavian poems known as the *Poetic Edda*.

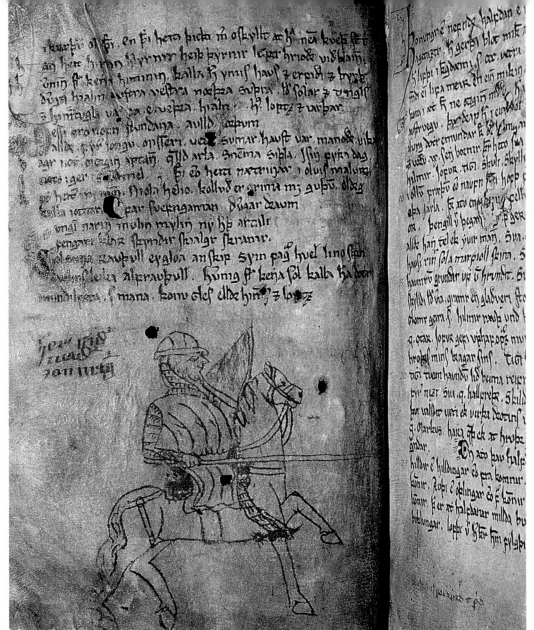

A warrior on horseback decorates the *Prose Edda*, one of our most important sources for the Norsemen's religious beliefs.

found evidence of human sacrifices. One ancient site in Denmark held the remains of several men who had been strangled and stabbed. The dead were probably slaves or prisoners of war sacrificed as an offering to the war god Odin.

In addition to their public observances, the Norsemen worshipped in their homes. A family often chose a god or goddess as their special protector and honored that deity through prayers and offerings. Farmers called on the nature spirits that were believed to inhabit the hills, rocks, and forests, asking for the spirits' help in their day-to-day lives. Warriors offered gifts to Odin before entering battle.

After the Viking kings of Denmark, Norway, and Sweden adopted Christianity, the Christian God gradually replaced the ancient Norse gods and goddesses. The Norse myths, which had been passed down orally for centuries, gave way to the ancient stories of the Bible. Before the traditional tales and poems of the Scandinavian people could be lost forever, however, Christian monks, priests, and scholars collected and recorded them. Thanks to their efforts, the beauty, humor, and excitement of Norse mythology would live on long after the end of the Viking Age.

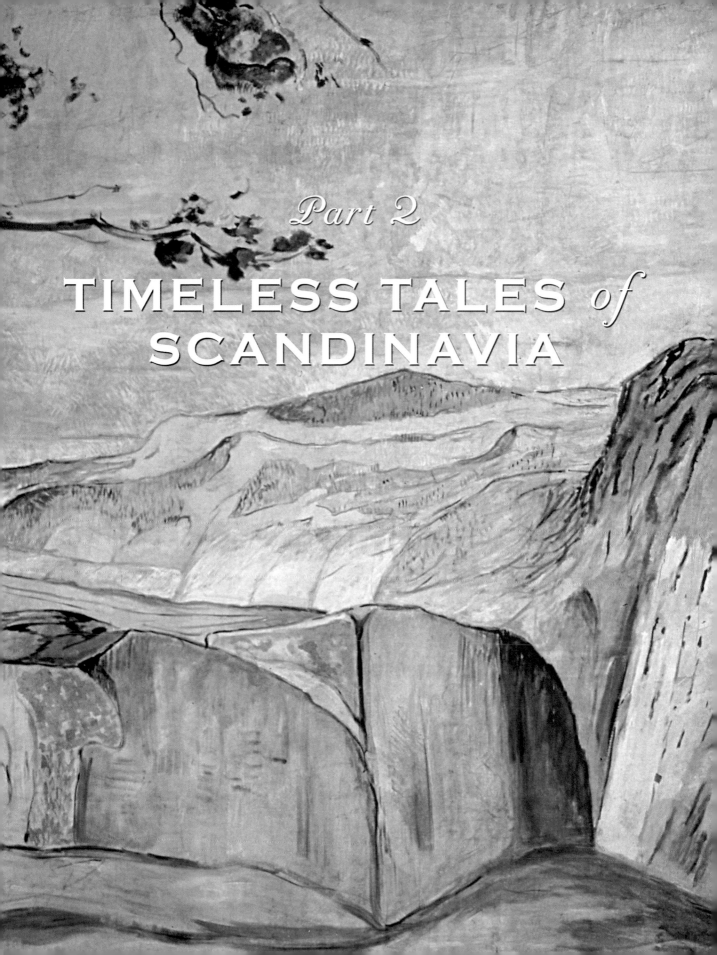

Part 2
TIMELESS TALES *of* SCANDINAVIA

THE BIRTH *of the* WORLDS

In the Beginning

THE NORSE MYTHS ARE LIKE EPISODES IN A LONG TALE packed with action, drama, and plenty of twists and turns. The tale begins at the beginning, with the creation of the universe. The Norsemen pictured the universe as a vast circle made up of three levels stacked one on top of the other like plates, with space in between. There were nine worlds on the three levels. A mighty ash tree called Yggdrasil, or the World Tree, grew through the center of them all. The Norse creation myth explains how the worlds and all their inhabitants, including gods, giants, and humans, came into existence.

Some parts of the Norse creation story are similar to myths from ancient India, Egypt, Persia (modern-day Iran), and other Eastern lands. The early Norsemen may have heard these accounts during foreign trading expeditions. Back home, skalds (courtly poets) told and retold the exotic tales, reshaping them to fit the land and character of Scandinavia. Icelandic poets recorded the first written versions around

Opposite: The world of Norse mythology is harsh and forbidding, much like the frozen expanses of Scandinavia.

Previous page: A storyteller passes on the ancient tales of Scandinavia, in a painting by the famous Norwegian artist Edvard Munch.

the end of the Viking Age. Their tales were set in a land of fiery volcanoes and massive glaciers, much like Iceland itself.

Our version of the Norse creation myth comes from two sources: the *Prose Edda* and the *Poetic Edda*. The *Prose Edda* is a handbook of Norse mythology written by Icelandic poet and historian Snorri Sturluson around 1220. Snorri was a devout Christian, but he had great respect for the culture of his ancestors. Concerned that this heritage was disappearing, he prepared a handbook that included his own retellings of many of the ancient myths that had been passed down orally for centuries. The *Poetic Edda* is a collection of thirty-four eddas (traditional Scandinavian poems of gods and heroes) composed by different poets at different times, some as early as the ninth century. The poems were written down by an unknown person or persons in Iceland sometime around the end of the thirteenth century. The Norse creation story is found in the eddic poem *Voluspa,* or "The Wise-Woman's Prophecy."

CAST *of* CHARACTERS

Ymir (EE-mir) First frost giant
Audhumla (OYD-hoom-lah) Sacred cow who freed the first god from the ice
Buri (BOOR-ee) First god; grandfather of the Aesir
Bor Son of Buri; father of Odin
Odin (OH-din) King of the gods
Vili (VILL-ih) and **Ve** (VEE) Odin's brothers
Bergelmir (BARE-gehl-mir) Grandson of Ymir
Ask (AHSK) and **Embla** (EM-blah) First man and woman

IN THE BEGINNING THERE WAS NO HEAVEN OR EARTH, no sand or sea or grass. There was only a land of frost in the north, a land of fire in the south, and a vast yawning void called Ginnunga-gap in between. Rivers flowed down from the land of frost. They hardened into ice, and great glaciers filled the northern part of Ginnunga-gap. Sparks and glowing embers flew up from the land of fire. They thawed the ice, making the southern part of the void golden and warm. Then, where sparks met frost, an amazing thing happened. Life appeared in the drops of water and grew into the likeness of a man. This creature was named Ymir, and he was the first of the frost giants.

Ymir fed on milk from a colossal cow called Audhumla, who had also formed from the melting ice. Audhumla fed by licking the salty ice blocks. By the evening of the first day, the cow's rough tongue had uncovered a man's hair. On the second day, a man's head appeared. On the third day, the whole man stepped free from the ice. He was called Buri, and he was the first of the gods.

In time Buri had a fine son named Bor. Bor married a giantess, and the couple had three sons, Odin, Vili, and Ve. The sons of Bor were handsome and strong and good. But Ymir, the frost giant, also had sons, and they were monstrous and evil. As might be expected, the two sides did not get along. In time their rivalry led to a battle. Odin and his brothers proved the more powerful. They slew the giant, and so much blood poured from the old ogre's wounds that the whole family of giants nearly drowned. Only the wise giant Bergelmir escaped. Grabbing his wife, he climbed into his boat, and they rode out the flood in safety. From Bergelmir and his wife would spring all the families of giants.

After the sons of Bor killed Ymir, they rolled him into the great void of Ginnunga-gap. Then they created the world from the giant's body. They pounded and pulled his flesh to fashion the Earth, with all its hills and plains and valleys. They made the mountains from his bones, the rocks and pebbles from his teeth, and the grass from his curly hair. They circled the Earth with the blood from Ymir's wounds, forming an ocean so vast that the very idea of crossing it would strike most men as impossible.

Next the gods took the giant's skull and raised it over the Earth to make the sky. They tossed his brains into the dome to make the billowing clouds. Then they gathered sparks from the land of flame to give light to the heavens. They placed the Sun and Moon and stars in the sky, fixing some in place and assigning others a path to travel.

> **THEY TOOK YMIR AND BORE HIM INTO THE MIDDLE OF THE YAWNING VOID, AND MADE OF HIM THE EARTH.**
>
> ~SNORRI STURLUSON, THE *PROSE EDDA*

Odin and his brothers were proud of their marvelous craftsmanship. The Earth and sky were beautiful. But somehow the universe still seemed empty. One day, as the gods were walking along the seashore, they came across two fallen trees. With his great powers, Odin raised the trees and breathed the spirit of life into them. Vili gave them movement and understanding. Ve bestowed the gifts of sight, speech, and hearing. When the brothers' work was finished, the new beings no longer looked like trees but like smaller versions of the gods themselves. Odin named the man Ask ("Ash") and the woman Embla ("Elm"). From this first man and woman all the races of men are descended.

The gods knew that all creatures need their own lands to settle. So they took Ymir's eyebrows and built a tall enclosure around the center of the Earth. They named this fortress Midgard and gave it to Ask and Embla for their home. They gave the land of Nidavellir ("Dark Fields") to the dwarfs, cunning creatures they had made from the maggots that bred in the Earth. They set aside Niflheim, below Midgard, for the dead. They gave Jotunheim, on the far edge of the ocean, to the

HOW THE SUN *and* MOON CROSS THE SKY

In the *Prose Edda,* Snorri Sturluson explains that our system of measuring the days and years began when the gods gave some of the heavenly bodies paths to travel. Odin and his brothers made special horse-drawn chariots to guide the Sun and Moon along their assigned paths. Then they visited the world of men to find drivers for their magical chariots.

There was a man called Mundilfari who had two children. They were so fair and beautiful that he called one of them Moon and the other, a daughter, Sun. . . . The gods, however, were angered at his arrogance and took the brother and sister and put them up in the sky. They made Sun drive the horses which drew the chariot of the sun that the gods had made to light the worlds. . . . Moon governs the journeying of the moon and decides the time of its waxing and waning. . . . [Sun] goes at a great pace; her pursuer is close behind her and there is nothing she can do but flee. . . . There are two wolves, and the one pursuing her who is called Skoll [Treachery] is the one she fears; he will catch her [at the end of the world]. The other that runs in front of her, however, is called Hati [Hater], . . . and he wants to catch the moon and will in the end.

Above: Two giant wolves pursue the Sun and Moon across the sky.

The NINE WORLDS *and* THEIR INHABITANTS

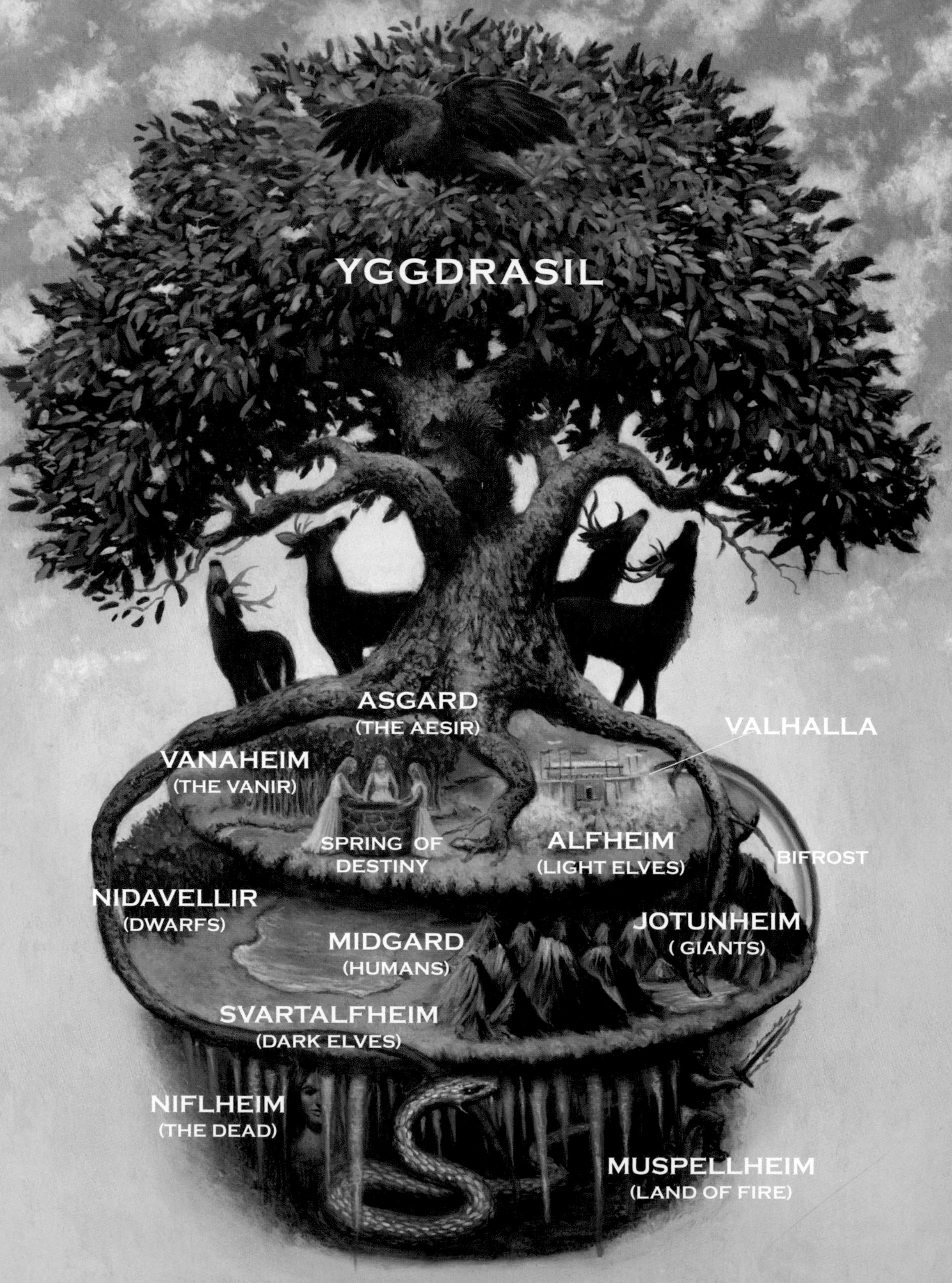
YGGDRASIL
ASGARD
(THE AESIR)
VALHALLA
VANAHEIM
(THE VANIR)
SPRING OF
DESTINY
ALFHEIM
(LIGHT ELVES)
BIFROST
NIDAVELLIR
(DWARFS)
JOTUNHEIM
(GIANTS)
MIDGARD
(HUMANS)
SVARTALFHEIM
(DARK ELVES)
NIFLHEIM
(THE DEAD)
MUSPELLHEIM
(LAND OF FIRE)

giants. Muspellheim, the land of fire, went to a fire giant named Surt, who guarded it with his flaming sword. The gods also fashioned other worlds, for the dark elves, the light elves, and the race of gods known as the Vanir.

Last of all, the gods built a stronghold for themselves above Midgard. They named it Asgard, or "Home of the Aesir." Here Odin sat on his high seat, watching over the nine worlds. He knew all that happened and understood all that he saw. Here Odin's wife Frigg and all his sons and daughters dwelt in magnificent halls with roofs of gold and rooms beyond number. There were twelve divine gods and twelve divine goddesses. All were sacred and powerful. But Odin was the highest of them all, and the others honored him as children do their father. So that Odin and his kindred could visit the world of humans, they built a bridge called Bifrost, connecting Asgard and Midgard. You have probably seen this marvelous flaming bridge, but you may call it the rainbow.

> AN ASH I KNOW,
> YGGDRASIL ITS NAME, . . .
> GREEN BY [THE] WELL
> DOES IT EVER GROW.
> ⁓VOLUSPA, *THE POETIC EDDA*

Supporting all the regions of the world was Yggdrasil, the greatest of all trees. This mighty ash had three immense roots, reaching into Asgard, Jotunheim, and Niflheim. It was tended by three fair maidens called the Norns. Each day these maidens, whose names were Past, Present, and Future, drew water from the Spring of Destiny, which flowed under the root in Asgard. They sprinkled the sacred water on the root of the tree so that its branches would not wither.

And so the nine worlds were created, and the great World Tree held them together. The divine Aesir sat on their thrones and held councils in heaven. There was peace and plenty, so that men called it the Golden Age. But, like all things, that blessed age was destined to end.

THE END *of the* GOLDEN AGE

Rebuilding Asgard's Wall

ACCORDING TO MYTHOLOGY, THE GOLDEN AGE THAT followed creation came to an end with the world's first war. It is not clear what started the conflict between the Aesir, the gods of war, and the Vanir, the gods of fertility who lived in the land of Vanaheim. We do know that the battle raged for long ages, ending only when the gods grew weary of fighting and declared a truce. To cement the peace, a few of the Vanir came to live with the Aesir in Asgard. They included Njord, god of the sea; Frey, god of the harvest; and Freyja, goddess of love and fertility.

In the myth "Rebuilding Asgard's Wall," we learn that the barrier that once surrounded the home of the Aesir was destroyed during the great war. A giant disguised as a stonemason offers to build a new wall for a high price: the Sun, the Moon, and the goddess Freyja. The gods scheme to gain the builder's work for free, but their plans soon unravel, with results that are nearly disastrous. Our retelling of this

Opposite:
A giant cowers in terror as Thor attacks a deadly sea serpent.

story is based on Snorri Sturluson's *Prose Edda,* the only surviving source that contains the complete myth.

The story of Asgard's wall is one of the first episodes in a series of Norse myths revolving around the hostility between the gods and giants. In these tales the gods represent the forces of order and good, while the giants stand for chaos and evil. If the giant stonemason succeeds in taking the Sun, the Moon, and Freyja, he will plunge the Earth into eternal darkness, bringing an end to the natural order of the seasons.

This myth also introduces one of the most complex and entertaining characters in Norse mythology, Loki. This unpredictable trickster is the son of a giant, but he lives with the gods in Asgard. Loki is handsome, clever, and mischievous. His cunning schemes place the gods in many difficult situations. However, he is also famous for using his wits to rescue them from their predicaments.

CAST *of* CHARACTERS

Freyja (FRAY-yuh) Goddess of love and fertility
Loki (LOW-kee) Trickster who lives in Asgard
Svadilfari (SVAHD-ill-fah-ree) Stallion who fathered Sleipnir
Thor God of thunder and lightning
Odin (OH-din) King of the gods
Sleipnir (SLAPE-nir) Odin's eight-legged horse

THE GODS WERE UNEASY. The terrible war between the Aesir and Vanir had left the great wall around Asgard in ruins. That left the stronghold of the gods wide open to attacks from the evil rock giants and frost giants. Still, despite the danger, no one volunteered for the wearisome job of rebuilding the massive wall.

One day a stonemason rode across the flaming bridge Bifrost on a magnificent stallion. The man offered to build a new wall, stronger and higher than ever. He would build such a wall that the realm of the gods would stay safe even if the giants stormed their way right up to Asgard's borders. But the mason demanded a heavy price for his services: the hand of the goddess Freyja in marriage and the Sun and the Moon as a bonus.

The gods were outraged by the mason's presumption. Freyja was wise and beautiful, the most renowned of all the goddesses. How dare a lowly builder even dream of marrying such a radiant being! As they

The rainbow bridge Bifrost connected Asgard with the world of humans.

spluttered and shouted, Loki's voice rose above the clamor. With a cunning smile, the trickster pointed out that it would take a year or more for the stonemason to build such a splendid structure. Why not agree to the man's terms, on the condition that he complete the task in a single winter? On the first day of summer, with the job still unfinished, the builder would forfeit his prize and the gods would gain part of a wall in the bargain.

What a brilliant idea! The gods took Loki's advice and presented the offer to the mason. The man agreed to strike the bargain, but only if his horse, Svadilfari, could help with the building. The gods looked at Loki. The sly one winked and shrugged. And so the gods and the mason took solemn oaths to bind them to their contract.

The first day of winter arrived, and the mason went right to work. Soon the gods were sorry they had listened to Loki. The builder's great stallion was more powerful than anyone could have imagined. Each night Svadilfari hauled incredibly huge boulders to his master. The next day the man shaped the rocks and fit them into the wall. As the weeks flew by, the stronghold grew higher and longer. The snows of winter began to melt, and the job neared completion. Three days before the start of summer, all that remained to build was the gateway, which the mason would surely complete on time with the help of his marvelous stallion.

Now the gods called another meeting. They debated for hours but could find no way out of their dilemma. The oaths they had taken were sacred. Breaking them would bring dishonor. Whose idea had it been, anyway, to accept that dreadful bargain and risk losing the Sun and

LOKI *the* TRICKSTER

The trickster is a common figure in mythology. The ancient Greeks, the Native Americans, and a number of other ancient peoples told stories about these contradictory characters who were sometimes charming and mischievous, sometimes cunning and cruel. Many tricksters were shape-shifters, able to take on the form of an animal or another person. Some could even change from male to female and give birth to children. Here is how the *Prose Edda* introduces Loki, one of the most famous mythological tricksters.

Also reckoned amongst the gods is one that some call the mischiefmonger of the Aesir and the father-of-lies and the disgrace-of-gods-and-men. He is the son of the giant Fárbauti and his name is Loki. . . . Loki is handsome and fair of face, but has an evil disposition and is very changeable of mood. He excelled all men in the art of cunning, and he always cheats. He was continually involving the Aesir in great difficulties and he often helped them out again by guile.

Loki could be charming as well as cunning and cruel.

Moon and Freyja? Slowly all eyes turned to Loki. With a deadly shout, all the gods swooped down on the troublemaker. Loki was scared out of his wits! Begging for mercy, he swore that, no matter what it cost him, he would make sure the mason lost his wages.

That evening, as the builder led his stallion toward the rock quarry, a dainty white horse trotted from the woods and whinnied invitingly.

Thor destroyed the rock giant with a blow from his magic hammer.

Loki had used his magical powers to change himself into a mare! One look at the lovely female and Svadilfari broke free from his master. The mare raced away and the stallion followed, with the builder lumbering after them. All that night the two horses galloped madly among the trees. No stones were hauled, and the mason could not work on the gateway.

The next two evenings, the mare appeared again. Once more there was no building. By the morning of the third day, the mason could see that he would never finish his work on time. He knew that the gods had tricked him. Seething with anger, he swelled up larger and larger, until suddenly he erupted. His disguise burst, and the gods saw that the stonemason was really a big, hulking, bellowing rock giant!

At the sight of their age-old enemy, the gods forgot their oaths. They hollered for Thor, and the thunder god came running with his mighty hammer. Thor paid the builder his wages, but it wasn't the Sun and the Moon and the goddess. Instead, the god cracked the rock giant's head open with a single blow from his hammer. Then Odin sent the giant down to Niflheim, where the souls of the dead dwell in darkness.

> THOR PAID THE BUILDER HIS WAGES, AND IT WAS NOT THE SUN AND MOON.
> ⁓SNORRI STURLUSON,
> THE *PROSE EDDA*

The summer months passed, and the gods completed the wall around Asgard. They sometimes wondered what had ever become of Loki, who had not been seen since winter. Then one day the trickster reappeared, leading an unusual gray colt with eight spindly legs. Loki the mare had given birth to the son of the stallion! To make sure the gods forgave his part in the unfortunate incident of the giant mason, Loki gave the marvelous colt to Odin. The king of gods named the horse Sleipnir. In time Sleipnir would grow to become the swiftest of all horses, carrying his master through the air, across the sea, down to the realm of the dead, and back again.

THE CYCLE *of the* SEASONS

Idun and the Magic Apples

IDUN, WHOSE NAME MEANS "REJUVENATOR" OR "RENEWER," was a Norse goddess of youth and fertility. She may originally have been one of the Vanir. The Aesir welcomed her to Asgard not only for her sweetness and beauty but also because she brought a wonderful gift. Idun had a basket of golden apples that gave whoever ate them eternal youth.

Idun reserved her apples for the gods and goddesses of Asgard. Naturally, that infuriated the giants, who wanted the gift of youth for themselves. In "Idun and the Magic Apples," a giant kidnaps the goddess and takes her to his mountain home in the north. Robbed of Idun's treasures, the Aesir become old and gray. As often happens in Norse mythology, it turns out that Loki the trickster was behind the gods' crisis, and it is Loki who must save them from their fate.

To the ancient Norsemen, this story might have explained the natural cycle of the seasons. When the golden goddess of youth is carried

Opposite: In this modern-day painting, Idun looks remarkably calm for a young goddess in the clutches of a giant eagle.

away to the frozen north, the winter winds howl and even the gods wither. Then Loki sweeps in like the south wind to restore Idun, along with all the beauty and renewal of spring. The myth also tells us why, unlike humans, the gods never grow old.

The myth of Idun's apples is found in two sources. Snorri Sturluson gives us the more recent version in the *Prose Edda*. Snorri based his retelling partly on a poem called *Haustlöng*, or "Autumn-Long," which was composed by Thjódólf of Hvin around the late ninth century. Thjódólf was skald, or court poet, to Harald Fairhair, the first king of a united Norway.

CAST *of* CHARACTERS

Odin (OH-din) King of the gods
Loki (LOW-kee) Trickster who lives in Asgard
Hoenir (HY-nir) Brother of Odin; sometimes known as Vili
Thiassi (THY-ah-see) Giant who kidnaps Idun
Idun (IH-doon) Goddess of youth, fertility, and the spring
Freyja (FRAY-yuh) Goddess of love and fertility
Heimdall (HAME-doll) Guardian of the bridge Bifrost

O NE FINE SUMMER MORNING, Odin, Loki, and Hoenir went exploring in the world of humans. All day long the three gods rambled across Midgard, climbing tall mountains and hiking through stony deserts. By the time the chariot of the Sun reached the western sky, their bellies were rumbling with hunger. Peering down into a green valley, the gods saw a herd of oxen. They killed a hefty ox, built a roaring fire, and placed the meat in the flames to cook it. Mouths drooling, they waited. After a time they pulled their supper out of the fire, but to their surprise, the meat was not ready. Again they built up the flames. They waited and waited. But when they tried the meat a second time, it was still raw. At that, Odin the wise declared, "There is dark magic at work here." And a voice above their heads answered, "It is my doing."

Gazing up in surprise, the companions saw a gigantic eagle perched in an oak tree. "Give me my fill of the ox, and I will let the fire cook it," said the eagle. The hungry gods agreed to the bargain. But when the bird sailed down from the tree and seized nearly the whole carcass, Loki grew angry. Grabbing a long, pointed stick, he stabbed the greedy creature. The bird flew up into the air with the weapon lodged in its breast. Then Loki found to his horror that his hands were stuck by magic to the other end of the stick.

The eagle flew off, towing the unlucky Loki behind it.

Swiftly the eagle coursed over the ground. It flew just low enough for Loki's legs to slam into every rock, tree stump, and thornbush. The desperate trickster felt as though his arms were being pulled from their sockets. He cried out to the eagle, begging for mercy. Then the great bird, who was really the giant Thiassi in disguise, said that he would let his victim go, on one condition. Loki must swear an oath to bring the goddess Idun and her apples of youth out of Asgard.

In a heartbeat the trickster agreed. Just as quickly, the giant released him, and Loki tumbled to the ground. With a few juicy curses, he picked himself up and limped back to Asgard. There he paid a visit to Idun's garden, where sweet birds sang and fragrant flowers bloomed in an eternal spring. The fair goddess was sitting beside a clear pool, a basket of shining apples in her lap. Smiling charmingly, Loki told Idun that he had found a wondrous tree just outside Asgard's borders. "It bears golden apples that look much like yours," said the trickster. "I will gladly show you the spot. Why not bring your basket, so that you may compare the fruit to your own apples?"

The young and trusting goddess gladly agreed. She gave Loki her hand, and the schemer led her out from the shelter of her garden, across the rainbow bridge Bifrost. The moment Idun set foot in Midgard, Thiassi swooped down on eagle's wings. Seizing the frightened girl with his claws, he leaped back into the sky. Then he carried her away to his home in the northern mountains.

> ALL [THE GODS] BECAME OLD AND GREY IN THEIR ASSEMBLY.
> ⁓THJÓDÓLF OF HVIN, *HAUSTLÖNG*

The next morning Odin found a gray hair on his pillow. Freyja gazed in her mirror and shrieked when she saw her first wrinkle. All the gods and goddesses hurried to Idun's garden for a bite of her enchanted apples. What they saw there made their hearts sink. Not only was the goddess missing, but the birds had fallen silent and all the lovely flowers were wilting.

That summer was the gloomiest ever in Asgard. Day by day the Aesir watched their youth and vitality fade away. Their hair turned gray. Their skin sagged and wrinkled. Their backs bent, and their limbs grew stiff and weary. At last Odin called an assembly. The once-mighty gods and goddesses shuffled to their thrones and spoke with trembling voices. Where could Idun have gone? Who had been the last to see her? Finally, Heimdall the watchman thumped the ground with his cane. "My memory is not what it used to be," he said, "but I believe that I last saw her crossing Bifrost, with Loki."

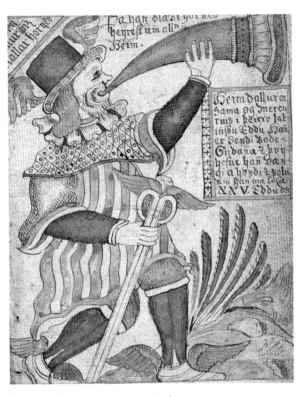

Heimdall, guardian of the rainbow bridge Bifrost, was the last to have seen Idun.

Roaring like an aged bear, Odin called for Loki's capture. The scoundrel was dragged before the assembly, and all the gods and goddesses quarreled over who should have the first chance to torture him. The frightened trickster fell to his knees, swearing that he would somehow retrieve Idun and her apples. He begged Freyja to lend him her magic feather coat, which she sometimes used to visit the land of the dead. Loki put on the coat and turned into a falcon. With a rude squawk, the little bird took off and flew north toward the land of giants.

All this time Idun had been pining away in the icy mountain home of Thiassi. Each day the giant demanded a bite of her magic apples. Each night he stormed and raged because she refused him. One morning Thiassi went hunting, leaving the unhappy goddess locked in a small, chilly room. Suddenly Loki whisked through the window. Landing on Idun's shoulder, he murmured magic words that Odin had given him and transformed her into a tiny brown nut. Then the little bird picked up the nut with his claws and headed back toward Asgard as fast as his wings could carry him.

When Thiassi came home and discovered that Idun was gone, he let out a howl that shook the snow from the mountaintops. The giant hurled himself into the air. He flapped his mighty eagle wings and hurried after the falcon. Back in Asgard, Odin looked up from his high seat. His far-seeing eyes spied the falcon and the giant eagle gaining on him. Odin shouted for the gods to pile wood shavings just inside Asgard's wall. The moment Loki sped over the wall, they thrust a torch into the fuel. The flames roared skyward. The huge eagle was caught in the blaze. His feathers caught fire, and Thiassi the giant plunged to the ground, where the gods took great pleasure in slaying him.

The gods visit Idun's garden for a taste of her magic apples.

After the commotion died down, Loki placed the nut on the ground. He said the magic words, and Idun stood before them. With a radiant smile, the goddess held up her basket of apples. As the Aesir tasted the fruit, the years melted away, and once more they stood strong and young and handsome.

To celebrate the glad occasion, the gods held a great feast among the flowers blossoming in Idun's garden. Then Odin, who was too happy to hold a grudge against anyone, threw Thiassi's eyes into the sky. There they would shine as two bright stars for as long as the world lasted.

ODIN'S QUEST *for* WISDOM

Many Norse myths tell of the wisdom of Odin. The king of gods was said to have spoken to the dead, plucked out one of his eyes, and even hanged himself on Yggdrasil in his endless quest for knowledge. The story of Odin's sacrifice on the World Tree is related in the poem *Hávamál,* or "The Speech of the High One," from the collection of traditional Scandinavian poems known as the *Poetic Edda.* In this excerpt from *Hávamál,* Odin explains that he sacrificed himself in order to learn the secret of runes. Runes were the characters, or letters, of the alphabet of the early Scandinavians. Used in short inscriptions on wood, stone, and other hard surfaces, they were often believed to have magical powers.

Above: Odin gave up one of his eyes in exchange for the gift of wisdom.

I know that I hung,
on a wind-rocked tree,
nine whole nights,
with a spear wounded,
and to Odin offered,
myself to myself;
on that tree,
of which no one knows
from what root it springs.

Bread no one gave me,
nor a horn of drink,
downward I peered,
to runes applied myself,
wailing learnt them,
then fell down thence. . . .

Then I began to bear fruit,
and to know many things,
to grow and well thrive:
word by word
I sought out words,
fact by fact
I sought out facts.

Thor Loses His Hammer

ODIN WAS THE KING OF THE GODS, BUT HIS SON THOR was just as highly honored. The strongest of all the gods, Thor had piercing eyes, a bristling red beard, and a lightning-quick temper. He was the only god who never rode on horseback, probably because of his great size. Instead, Thor drove a huge chariot pulled by two gigantic goats. Lightning flashed from the goats' hooves and the wheels of the chariot sounded like thunder whenever the god rolled across the heavens.

Thor's greatest pleasure in life was battling giants. A number of myths recount his exploits in Jotunheim, the land of the giants, where he overcame great obstacles to defeat his foes. His favorite weapon was a magic hammer called Mjollnir ("Crusher"). When Thor hurled his red-hot hammer, it became a thunderbolt. Mjollnir never missed its mark, and it always returned to its owner.

The myth "Thor Loses His Hammer" is found in *Thrymskvida* ("The Poem of Thrym"), composed in Iceland sometime between the tenth

Opposite: Thor storms across the heavens, lightning flashing from his powerful hammer.

and early thirteenth centuries and preserved in the *Poetic Edda*. In *Thrymskvida*, the thunder god discovers that Thrym, king of the frost giants, has stolen Mjollnir. With Loki as his companion, Thor sets out for Jotunheim to recover his prized hammer. In order for his quest to succeed, the big, bearded, muscular god must disguise himself as a beautiful goddess. There are no special hidden meanings in this comical tale. The Norsemen told it just for fun.

CAST *of* CHARACTERS

Thor God of thunder and lightning
Loki (LOW-kee) Trickster who lives in Asgard
Freyja (FRAY-yuh) Goddess of love and fertility
Thrym (THRIM) King of the frost giants

ONE MORNING Thor awoke and rubbed the sleep from his eyes. He reached for his magic hammer. Mjollnir was gone!

With a roar that shook the nine worlds, Thor called for Loki. For once, though, the mischief maker was innocent. Even Loki would not dare steal the mighty hammer that alone kept the terrible frost giants from storming Asgard.

Thor paced up and down, yanking his fiery red beard. Loki sat and pondered. At last the clever trickster had an idea. "Only the giants could commit such a dastardly crime," he said. "I will ask Freyja for her

Opposite: Freyja's most prized possessions were her magic falcon cloak and her precious jeweled necklace.

magic falcon cloak, so that I may fly to Jotunheim and find the thief."

Thor and Loki hurried to Freyja's chambers. When the lovely goddess heard that Thor's hammer was missing, she turned pale with worry. Without hesitation she wrapped her feathered cloak around Loki, transforming him into a falcon.

Swiftly the little bird winged its way to chilly Jotunheim. There Loki saw Thrym, king of the frost giants, sitting alone on a mountaintop.

"How are things in the land of gods?" asked the giant politely.

"Very bad," replied Loki. "Someone has stolen Thor's hammer."

"I stole the hammer," answered Thrym with an evil laugh that froze Loki to the marrow. "What's more, I have hidden it eight miles down in the Earth, where no man or god shall ever find it. If Thor wants to see his precious Mjollnir again, he must send me fair Freyja as my wife."

In a whirl of feathers, Loki raced back to Asgard with the news. Again he and Thor hurried to Freyja's chambers. This time the goddess was not so cooperative. In fact, when she heard Thrym's proposal, she flew into a rage. Never *never* NEVER would Freyja marry that big, ugly giant!

Now all the Aesir gathered together to discuss the perilous situation. They turned over one plan after another. Finally, they came up with a solution. They would dress Thor as a bride and send him in place of Freyja.

"I won't do it!" Thor howled. "I will look like a sissy!" But the gods and goddesses ignored his protests. Struggling to hide their smiles, they bundled the burly thunder god into a wedding dress. They slipped gold bands on his hairy arms and clasped Freyja's jeweled necklace around his thick neck. A long white bridal veil covered his beard. A pretty cap topped his shaggy head. Loki gleefully dressed up as the maid to the blushing bride. Then off the pair went in Thor's goat-drawn chariot.

Thunder shook the mountains and fire split the clouds as Thor's chariot drew near Jotunheim. When Thrym heard the racket, he shouted for his servants. "Make haste and prepare a great feast," the giant ordered joyfully. "The gods have sent the greatest of all treasures, fair Freyja, to be my wife!"

Soon the happy groom escorted his bride to the banquet hall. He watched in pride as the veiled maiden took her seat among the giant guests at the table. Then his jaw dropped. His future wife had grabbed an entire ox! After gobbling that down, she ate eight whole salmon and all the other dainties prepared for the ladies, washing down the feast with three vats of mead.

"Who has ever seen a maiden with such hunger and thirst?" the giant asked in amazement.

"It is a sign of her passion," said Loki the bridesmaid in a high, squeaky voice. "My mistress was so eager for the wedding that she has not eaten a morsel in eight days."

Hearing that, the giant grew more excited than ever. He bent toward his bride and lifted a corner of her veil for a kiss. With a gasp Thrym jumped back as if struck by a thunderbolt. "Freyja's eyes are so bright and fierce," he cried. "They seem to burn like fire!"

"It is a sign of her desire," said the clever bridesmaid. "My mistress was so eager for the wedding that she has not slept in eight nights."

Now Thrym practically swooned with love for his remarkable bride. He called for his servants to bring forth Mjollnir, for all proper weddings must be blessed with Thor's hammer. "Lay the hammer in the maiden's lap," cried the king of the giants, "to seal our marriage oaths and ensure blessings on our union."

Mjollnir was brought from its hiding place. When Thor felt his trusty hammer in his lap, his heart leaped within him. Thrym reached for his bride's hand. He got the surprise of his life when a big hairy arm loomed up over his head, swinging the weapon. Thor tore off his veil and cracked the giant's skull with the hammer. He sang as he clobbered all the other guests at the bridal banquet. Then Thor and Loki strode to the chariot and drove back to Asgard, where all the gods and goddesses sighed in relief at the sight of the precious hammer.

THE NORSEMEN SPEAK
FOR *the* HONOR *of* THOR

Thor was the most popular of all the Norse gods. The early Scandinavians prayed and made sacrifices to ensure his blessings on their homes, crops, and families. Many men and women showed their devotion to the hammer-wielding god by wearing miniature metal hammers on chains around their necks. A sacred hammer or the sign of the hammer was also used to bless brides, newborn children, and the dead. In addition, Thor was honored with statues in many temples built during Viking times. *Flateyjarbók* ("Flat Island Book"), a collection of dramatic tales written in Iceland in the late 1300s, describes a statue of the beloved god found at a temple in Norway.

> Thor sat in the middle. He was the most highly honored. He was huge, and all adorned with gold and silver. Thor was arranged to sit in a chariot; he was very splendid. There were goats, two of them, harnessed in front of him, very well wrought. Both car and goats ran on wheels. The rope round the horns of the goats was of twisted silver, and the whole was worked with extremely fine craftsmanship.

The Binding of Fenrir the Wolf

IN THE STORY OF THOR'S HAMMER AND MANY OTHER Norse myths, the gods used their strength and wits to triumph over the giants. The Norsemen also told a number of tales in which the gods suffered losses. One of the best-known of these darker myths was the story of Fenrir the wolf. The only complete account of this myth is found in Snorri Sturluson's *Prose Edda*.

According to Snorri, a lady giant once caught the eye of Loki the trickster. From Loki's union with the giantess came three monstrous children: an immense snake called the Midgard Serpent, a hideous woman called Hel, and the fierce wolf Fenrir. In time Fenrir grew so huge and powerful that no ordinary chain could bind him. The gods obtained a magic bond to control the menacing beast. They managed to place the chain on Fenrir, but Tyr, god of war, lost his hand in the process.

Wolves were an ever-present danger in the lives of the early Scandinavians, so it is not surprising that they play a role in the Norse

Opposite:
Courageous Tyr sacrifices his hand so that his fellow gods can bind Fenrir the wolf.

myths. As the most terrible of all the mythological wolves, Fenrir represents the destructive forces of nature. Raised among the gods in Asgard, he is also a symbol of the hatred, greed, and violence that can reside within the self. By enabling his fellow gods to restrain Fenrir, Tyr saves the world from destruction. He also saves the gods from the dark forces that can corrupt from within, overpowering reason and destroying the spirit. Tyr's actions reflect the highest ideals of the Norse warrior. He faces his enemy with courage and endures the loss of his hand without complaint. But the gods' victory is just one battle in a long war. According to prophecies, Fenrir will break his bonds and fight on the side of the giants in the final battle of Ragnarok.

CAST *of* CHARACTERS

Loki (LOW-kee) Trickster who lives in Asgard

Odin (OH-din) King of the gods

Midgard Serpent Giant serpent who encircles the Earth

Hel Goddess of death and the underworld

Fenrir (FEN-rir) Giant wolf fathered by Loki

Tyr (TEER) God of war and justice

Frey (FRAY) God of sunshine, rain, peace, prosperity, and the harvest

Skirnir (SKEER-nir) Frey's servant

ONE DAY disturbing news reached Asgard. Loki the trickster had fathered three children in the land of the frost giants. The first was a snapping wolf cub. The second was a spitting serpent. The third was a grim-looking hag whose body was half pink and wholesome, half black and decayed.

Now, Loki was trouble enough by himself. What evil might arise from his monstrous children? In search of an answer, the gods traveled to the home of the Norns, beside the Spring of Destiny, in the shadow of the World Tree. What the three maidens told them was anything but reassuring. For it was destined that Loki's children would bring the gods terrible harm and sorrow.

As soon as they heard the Norns' prophecy, the gods captured the three young monsters. Odin flung the serpent into the sea that surrounded Midgard, where it grew so large that it encircled the entire world of humans. Next the king of gods cast the hag down into the dark underworld. There she became known as Hel, queen of the dead. From then on, the souls of all who died of sickness, accident, or old age instead of glorious battle went to Hel's dreary domain. There they dined in her hall Damp-with-Sleet, at a table called Hunger, surrounded by tapestries called Glimmering Misfortune.

Thor is destined to battle the Midgard Serpent at Ragnarok, the final battle at the end of the world.

Finally Odin turned to the wolf cub Fenrir. The Norns had said that this beast was the most dangerous of Loki's children. Therefore Odin decided that the wolf should be raised in Asgard, where the gods could keep an eye on him.

It was not long before Odin began to regret his decision. Within a day the cub was the size of a full-grown wolf. Within a week his huge head towered over the golden rooftops of Asgard. The beast snarled and flashed his massive fangs whenever anyone approached him. Soon none of the gods dared to feed him, except Odin's brave son Tyr. Each day Tyr gave Fenrir huge joints of meat, which the greedy wolf devoured bones and all. And each day Fenrir grew larger and stronger and more ferocious.

The gods had to find a way to restrain Fenrir before it was too late. So they made a heavy brass chain and asked the wolf to try it on as a test of his strength. With a sneer the monster agreed. The moment the gods bound him, he stretched and easily broke the chain. Next the gods forged a massive iron chain, with links twice as strong as the first. Again they challenged Fenrir, declaring that anyone strong enough to break such a chain would gain fame throughout the nine worlds. Fenrir allowed the gods to bind him. This time he had to strain and struggle, but again he shattered the chain.

> THEY MADE A VERY STRONG FETTER . . . AND BROUGHT IT BEFORE THE WOLF, BIDDING HIM TRY HIS STRENGTH.
> — SNORRI STURLUSON, THE *PROSE EDDA*

At last, the gods realized that no ordinary chain could bind Fenrir. So Odin sent Frey's servant Skirnir down to the world of the dwarfs. Those cunning craftsmen fashioned a chain from six things: the sound of a cat's footsteps, the beard of a maiden, the roots of a mountain, the timidity of a bear, the voice of a fish, and the spit of a bird. The magic

The DWARFS WORK THEIR MAGIC

In Norse mythology a race of dwarfs lived underground in a land called Nidavellir, or "Dark Fields." Famed far and wide for their craftsmanship, the dwarfs made many fabulous treasures for the gods. In this passage from the *Prose Edda,* a dwarf named Eitri is hard at work forging Thor's famous hammer. His brother Brokk, who is working the bellows that fan the furnace fire, is tormented by a fly. The pest is none other than Loki, who has bet his head that Eitri will not complete his task. Although Loki loses the bet, he manages to save his head. In the end, though, the dwarf has the last laugh.

Then [Eitri] put iron in the furnace and told [Brokk] to blow, and said that everything would be spoiled if the bellows stopped working. . . . The fly settled between [Brokk's] eyes and stung him on the eyelids so that the blood ran into his eyes and he could not see at all. He stopped the bellows and as quickly as possible brushed the fly away with one hand. At that moment the smith came in and said that everything in the furnace had been within an ace of being spoiled. Then he took from the forge a hammer. . . .

[The gods] decided that [Eitri] had won the wager. Then Loki offered to redeem [buy back] his head but the dwarf said that he could not expect to do that. "Catch me, then!" said Loki, and when the dwarf tried to seize him he was already a long way off. . . . Then the dwarf asked Thor to catch him and he did so. The dwarf wanted to cut off his head, but Loki said he had a claim on his head but not his neck. The dwarf took a thong [leather cord] and a knife and . . . sewed up [Loki's] mouth.

This stone carving from Denmark shows Loki with his mouth stitched shut.

chain was as smooth and soft as a silk ribbon. But because it was made from ingredients that were not of this world, no power in the world could break it.

As soon as Skirnir returned with the magic cord, the gods took it to Fenrir. They challenged the wolf to once again prove his might. But this time Fenrir refused to be bound. The silken ribbon looked so slender and weak that no fame would come from breaking it. In fact, it looked so flimsy that Fenrir suspected a trick.

"If that cord has been made by magic," said the wolf, "it will never come off, slender though it may look."

"Very well, don't try it," said Odin with a scornful smile. "There is no shame in being afraid of the gods."

The wolf laid back his ears and growled. "I am no coward," he snarled. "I will let you bind me with that cord, but only if one of you puts his hand between my jaws as a sign of your good faith."

The gods looked at the wolf's long, sharp fangs. They looked at each other and shook their heads. Then, without a word, Tyr stepped forward, put out his right hand, and placed it in the wolf's mouth.

[TYR] IS MOST DARING, AND BEST IN STOUTNESS OF HEART.
~ SNORRI STURLUSON, THE *PROSE EDDA*

At once the gods wrapped the silken cord around Fenrir's neck and legs. The wolf began to struggle. The more he stretched and strained, the tighter the magic band became. Fenrir knew he was trapped. His eyes flashed with fury. All the gods laughed with relief—all except Tyr. He lost his hand.

When Fenrir opened his bloodstained jaws for another bite, one of the gods stuck in a sword. The hilt rested in the wolf's lower jaw and the point in the roof of his mouth. Then the gods tied one end of the magic chain to a giant boulder and shoved the rock deep down into the Earth. There the wolf would lie, howling through his gag, until the time of Ragnarok.

THE END *of* WINTER

Frey and the Giant Maiden

THE RELATIONSHIP BETWEEN THE GODS AND GIANTS was not always hostile. Several Norse myths speak of friendship, attraction, and even love between the two races. Both conflict and love play a part in the story of Frey and Gerd.

Frey was one of the Vanir, or fertility gods, who came to live with the Aesir after the great war of the gods. According to mythology, he had a wonderful horse that could leap through fire unharmed and a magic shining sword that fought giants by itself. But he gave up both of these treasures for the love of the giant maiden Gerd.

Frey had seen the beautiful but coldhearted Gerd from afar and fallen in love with her. He sent his faithful servant Skirnir to the world of the giants to win the maiden's heart. Skirnir tried to bribe Gerd with wonderful gifts. When that failed, he resorted to increasingly nasty threats. At last, the giantess agreed to meet Frey in a sacred grove in nine nights' time and become his bride.

Opposite:
Frey sat on Odin's high seat and beheld the beautiful giant maiden Gerd.

To the Norsemen, the myth of Frey and Gerd affirmed the natural order of the world. At the story's end, the beautiful giantess moves from the evil and chaotic world of the giants to the orderly world of the gods. According to some interpretations, the myth also may have explained the warming of the Earth by the Sun in springtime. Gerd, whose name means "Fenced-In," represents a wintry field. Through his messenger Skirnir, or "Shining," Frey sends the spring Sun. Frey's love eventually melts the maiden's heart, just as the Sun's rays thaw the frozen Earth.

Our retelling of the story of Frey and Gerd is based on two sources: the tenth-century poem *För Skírnis* ("Skirnir's Journey") from the *Poetic Edda* and Snorri Sturluson's *Prose Edda*.

CAST *of* CHARACTERS

Frey (FRAY) God of sunshine, rain, peace, prosperity, and the harvest

Njord (NYURD) God of the sea

Gymir (GIH-mir) Giant father of Gerd

Skirnir (SKEER-nir) Frey's servant

Gerd Giantess who marries Frey

FREY, SON OF NJORD, knew that no one was allowed on Odin's high seat except the king of gods and his queen. Still, the young god could not help wondering what it would be like to sit on that exalted seat and look out over all the nine worlds. One day Frey's curiosity got the better of him. He sneaked into the great god's hall and sat himself down on the throne.

How wonderful to see so clearly and so far! Frey turned his eyes to the frozen north and gasped as the land of the giants came into view. There on a mountaintop was the dwelling of the terrible giant Gymir. A beautiful young giantess was walking up a path to the hall. When the maiden raised her snow-white arms to open the door, her dazzling beauty lighted up the sky. Frey's heart swelled with longing. He rose and wandered home in a daze, so sick with love that he knew he had been well punished for sitting on Odin's throne.

For many long days, Frey moped in his hall. Sunlight faded from the Earth, and crops thirsted for rain. The gods grew more and more worried. Finally, Njord summoned his son's trusted servant Skirnir and asked him to seek out the cause of Frey's unhappiness.

Skirnir hastened to Frey's chambers. "Why do you sit here, alone and downcast?" he asked his master.

"I have seen a maiden dear to me, and I cannot live without her," the god groaned. "But I know my love is hopeless, for she is Gerd, Gymir's daughter, and her heart is surely as cold as winter."

"Do not despair," said Skirnir. "Though the journey to Jotunheim is long and dangerous, I will go there and woo the maiden for you. Only give me your horse that rides through fire and your gleaming sword that fights by itself."

Frey gladly granted Skirnir's wishes. Riding the wonderful horse and armed with the magic sword, the messenger fought his way through dark valleys and flickering flames to Jotunheim. At last he saw the hall of Gerd, Gymir's daughter. Huge hounds guarded the gates, snapping and howling like the chill winds of winter.

From inside her chambers, Gerd heard the racket. "What noise is that?" she asked her maidservant. "The ground shakes, and the house around me trembles."

"A man is riding up to the gates," said the servant. "He leaps from his horse. He draws near your father's fierce hounds."

"Bid the brave stranger enter, and offer him mead," ordered the fair giant maiden.

So Skirnir passed by the terrible hounds and entered Gerd's ice-cold chambers. He wasted no time getting to his errand. "I serve Frey, lord of Sunshine and life-giving rain," he told Gymir's daughter. "I will give you eleven golden apples if you will marry my master."

"You cannot buy me with apples," said the maiden in a voice as cold as snow. "There are treasures enough in my father's house, and I do not love your master."

Skirnir offered Gerd a wonderful gold ring, which spun off eight more rings just like it every ninth night.

"You cannot buy me with rings," said the maiden in a voice as hard as ice. "I

APPLES ALL-GOLDEN
I HAVE HERE ELEVEN:
THESE I WILL GIVE THEE,
GERD, THY LOVE TO GAIN.
⁓ FÖR SKÍRNIS, THE POETIC EDDA

have all the gold I need in my father's house, and I do not love your master."

Then Skirnir grew angry. He flourished Frey's shining sword. "Do you see what I hold in my hand?" he shouted. "I will cut off your head if you do not obey my master's summons."

"You cannot sway me with force," said the proud giant maiden. "You had best leave, before my father finds you here and slays you."

Now Skirnir used his last and most terrible weapon. Carving three magic runes on his staff, he pronounced the curse that would fall on Gerd if she persisted in her defiance. "The wrath of the gods be upon you," cried the shining messenger. "You shall dwell alone at the edge of heaven and gaze on Hel's gates forever. Your meat will taste vile. Filth will be your only drink. Your skin will rot away, and men will view you with loathing. Never shall you know a husband, though you go mad with loneliness and longing."

Shaken by the dreadful curse, Gerd filled a frosty cup with mead. Shedding icy tears, she offered it to Skirnir. "Find welcome here instead," said the giant maiden, "and a heart willing for your master."

Then Skirnir lowered his staff and erased the curse. Gerd pledged to meet Frey after nine nights, in the sacred forest of Barri ("Barley"). Joyfully the messenger rode home and found his anxious master waiting. He told Frey the glad tidings. But instead of rejoicing, the god moaned, "Nine nights! How shall I bear to wait when my heart is so filled with desire?"

Somehow Frey survived the long lonesome hours until his wedding. On the ninth night, the frost maiden kept her promise. When Gerd entered the sacred grove and saw her intended husband, the warmth of his love melted her cold heart. She took her seat beside Frey in Asgard, where they dwelled together in happiness. And on Earth the people enjoyed a season of peace, fine weather, and rich harvests.

THE
DESCENT of ODIN.

AN ODE.

Uprose the King of men with speed,
And saddled strait his coal-black steed;
Down the yawning steep he rode,
That leads to Hela's drear abode.
Him the dog of darkness spied;
His shaggy throat he opened wide,
While from his jaws, with carnage fill'd,
Foam and human gore distill'd.
Hoarse he brays with hideous din,
Eyes that glow, and fangs that grin;
And

THE DOOM *of the* GODS

Balder's Death and Ragnarok

ONE UNUSUAL FEATURE OF THE NORSE RELIGION WAS that the gods were not believed to be immortal. All of the "episodes" of Norse mythology lead up to Ragnarok, or "Doom of the Gods." This tragic end will come about through the actions of Loki the trickster. We have already seen that Loki is a contradictory character. In the earlier myths, he gets the gods in and out of trouble with his mischievous pranks. At heart, though, Loki is evil. By allowing this evil to remain in their midst, the gods end up losing their greatest treasure and sealing their doom.

The great treasure of the gods is Balder, pure and radiant lord of light and innocence. Jealousy leads Loki to trick Balder's blind brother, Hod, into causing the beloved god's death. Balder's downfall is a sign of the coming of Ragnarok. During this final battle between good and evil, the gods die fighting their ancient foes and the whole Earth is destroyed. But as foretold in prophecies, a new world cleansed of all evil is reborn from the destruction.

Opposite: Odin gallops down to the underworld, in an 18th-century illustration by the English artist, poet, and visionary William Blake.

The myths of Balder's death and Ragnarok are told in a number of Norse poems and prose narratives. The early Scandinavians may have borrowed some elements of these tales from the peoples of other cultures, including the Persians of ancient Iran and the Celts of central and western Europe. In addition, some scholars think that the Norse accounts of doomsday may have been influenced by the Christian vision of Judgment Day, as told in the book of Revelation. There are also distinctive features in the Norse myths that clearly reflect the land and character of early Scandinavia. Like the Norse creation story, Ragnarok takes place in a land of fire and flood. And like the ideal Scandinavian warrior, the gods face their enemies bravely, accepting their fate and laughing in the face of death.

CAST *of* CHARACTERS

Balder (BAWL-der) God of light, innocence, joy, purity, and beauty

Odin (OH-din) King of the gods

Hel Goddess of death and the underworld

Hod (HAWD) Blind god of darkness

Frigg Wife of Odin; queen of the Aesir

Thor God of thunder and lightning

Loki (LOW-kee) Trickster who lives in Asgard

Fenrir (FEN-rir) Giant wolf fathered by Loki

Midgard Serpent Giant serpent who encircles the Earth

Surt Fire giant who rules Muspellheim, the land of fire

Heimdall (HAME-doll) Guardian of the bridge Bifrost

Tyr (TEER) God of war and justice

Frey (FRAY) God of sunshine, rain, peace, prosperity, and the harvest

Balder's Dreams

BALDER, SON OF ODIN, was the best of the gods. His beauty lighted up the worlds, and his innocence and sweet disposition made all creation adore him. The gentle god lived in a fair hall called Broad-Gleaming, where no impure thoughts or visions ever crossed the threshold.

Then one night Balder began to have terrible dreams. Monsters chased him and threatened to cast him down into the darkness forever. When Balder told his father of his dreams, Odin was filled with foreboding. The king of gods saddled his wonderful eight-legged horse Sleipnir and rode down the long gloomy road to Hel's domain. Outside the gates he disguised his features and used his powerful charms to call up the spirit of a long-dead wisewoman. Odin asked the prophetess why Hel's halls were hung with gold ornaments. "The hall is decked, the table set, the mead brewed to welcome Balder," said the dreadful spirit.

Odin rides his eight-legged horse, Sleipnir.

Odin's heart sank. "What demon shall steal the life from Odin's son?" he demanded.

"Balder's own brother, blind Hod, shall be his bane," she answered.

Then Odin roared with grief, and the spirit saw through his disguise. "Ride home, king of gods, and come here no more," she cried with cruel laughter. "For the hope of the Aesir is gone, and destruction comes to Asgard."

With that awful pronouncement, the spirit sank back into her grave. Odin returned to Asgard with a heavy heart. He knew that what was fated must come to pass, and nothing in heaven or Earth could stop it. But he could not bring himself to tell the gods and goddesses that they would lose their beloved Balder.

The Death of Balder

Frigg made all the world's creatures swear an oath not to harm Balder.

THE AESIR WERE WORRIED about Balder's nightmares. They feared that the dreams were an omen, warning that the beloved god's life was in danger. While one god after another proposed plans to protect Balder, Odin sat silent. At last Frigg declared that she knew a way to guard her son from peril.

Frigg traveled to every corner of the nine worlds, visiting anything that could bring danger. She spoke with fire, water, earth, stones, metals, trees, beasts, birds, snakes, poisons, and every kind of illness. Each of these agreed to swear an oath that it would never harm Balder.

After Frigg completed her task, the Aesir put it to the test. Balder stood in their midst, and someone tossed a pebble at him. The tiny missile stopped in midair and fell to the ground. Next someone tossed a stick. It too fell harmlessly. Soon all the gods and goddesses were laughing merrily, enjoying their new game. One threw darts at the shining god. Another swung his sword. Thor even hurled his mighty hammer. No matter what they did, nothing could harm Balder.

But someone was not laughing. Loki the trickster sulked in a corner, jealousy gnawing at his black heart. The gods had been avoiding Loki, blaming him for all their troubles. Now they had the nerve to make a fuss over their golden-haired darling! Slipping away unnoticed, Loki transformed himself into a haggard old woman and hobbled over to Frigg's hall. "Do you hear that laughter?" he asked the goddess in a raspy old voice. "I wonder what the Aesir are up to."

"They are playing games with my son Balder," Frigg answered happily. "All the world loves him, and nothing can harm him."

"Nothing, good mother?" asked the old hag. "Has *everything* sworn an oath to spare him?"

"Everything but a little plant called mistletoe," said Frigg. "I found it growing on the trunk of an oak tree outside Odin's golden hall of Valhalla, but I thought it too young for oath taking."

Smiling slyly to himself, Loki bid the goddess good day. As he left her hall, he resumed his old form and hurried to Valhalla. There he found the mistletoe, just as Frigg had described it. He plucked a small sprig and sharpened it into a dart. Then he hurried back to the merry circle in Asgard. He sidled up to the blind god Hod, who stood apart from the others. "Why aren't you throwing things at your brother like everyone else?" asked Loki.

"Because I can't see him," Hod explained patiently. "Besides, I have no weapon."

"Here, take this little twig," said Loki. "I will show you where Balder is standing."

Loki tricks the blind god Hod into stabbing Balder with a mistletoe spear.

So Hod took his place among the gods and aimed where Loki directed. The sharp dart flew through the air. It pierced Balder through the heart. The golden god fell dead to the ground.

There was a moment of shocked silence. Then all the gods and goddesses began weeping. None was more overcome with grief than Odin. He alone knew what the loss of his dearest son meant for the Aesir. For Odin had looked into the future, and he knew that Balder's death was the first sign of Ragnarok.

Endings and Beginnings

AFTER THE DEATH OF BALDER, light and innocence left the Earth. Brother killed brother, father slew son, and sons rose up against their fathers. Everywhere was sin and misery, until Midgard ran red with blood. Then the gods knew that the prophecies of old were about to be fulfilled. Ragnarok was at hand.

As had been foretold, the Earth endured three years of winter without end. Snows fell, winds howled, and frost hardened the ground. Sun and Moon looked fearfully over their shoulders, and the wolves that had long pursued them caught and devoured them. The stars vanished

The GODS PUNISH LOKI

After Balder died, Hel declared that she would release the god from her grim domain if all creation wept for him. The Aesir sent messengers throughout the nine worlds. Men and beasts, fire and water, stones and metals all began weeping. Everything wept except one hard-hearted giantess, who turned out to be Loki in disguise. For this last act of treachery, the gods seized the trickster and bound him in a cave deep beneath the Earth.

This account of Loki's punishment comes from a prose note at the end of the tenth-century poem *Lokasenna,* or "Loki's Wrangling." The brief narrative mentions four little-known characters from Norse mythology: Loki's faithful wife, Sigyn; their two sons, Vali and Narfi; and Skadi, wife of the sea god Njord.

Loki hid himself in [a] waterfall in the guise of a salmon, and there the gods took him. He was bound with the bowels of his son Vali, but his son Narfi was changed to a wolf. Skadi took a poison-snake and fastened it up over Loki's face, and the poison dropped thereon. Sigyn, Loki's wife, sat there and held a shell under the poison, but when the shell was full she bore away the poison, and meanwhile the poison dropped on Loki. Then he struggled so hard that the whole earth shook therewith; and now that is called an earthquake.

Above: The gods devised a grim punishment for the treacherous Loki.

from the darkened sky. The Earth groaned and shuddered, until the trees were uprooted and great mountains tumbled down.

As the frozen Earth cracked open, all bonds were broken. The wolf Fenrir escaped from his long imprisonment. His eyes blazed with fire, and his huge mouth gaped open, with the lower jaw scraping the ground and the upper jaw pressed against the sky. The Midgard Serpent rose from the sea and slithered onto land, spitting poison. The sky burst asunder and out rode the giants, led by Surt and his bright sword of fire. The gates of Hel opened and the dead rose in arms, with Loki as their leader.

> ## AXE-TIME, SWORD-TIME, SHIELDS ARE SUNDERED, WIND-TIME, WOLF-TIME, ERE THE WORLD FALLS.
> ~ *VOLUSPA*, THE *POETIC EDDA*

From his post beside Bifrost, Heimdall saw the evil hosts advance on Asgard. He blew his great horn, calling the Aesir to the final battle. At that stirring sound, the gods sprang from their golden halls, strapped on their armor, and mounted their warhorses. Swiftly they galloped over the rainbow bridge, shouting their brave battle cries.

The two armies met on the vast plain called Vigrid, or "Battle Surge." There mighty Odin fought Fenrir but was swallowed up by the monster-wolf's jaws. Thor slew the Midgard Serpent, then staggered and fell, killed by the serpent's poisonous breath. Tyr died battling the hounds of Hel. Heimdall battled with Loki, and each killed the other. Frey struggled with Surt and died. Then Surt flung his fiery sword. The whole world was engulfed in flames, and the Earth sank into the boiling sea.

For long ages all was dark and silent. Then one day a new Earth rose from the sea. It was green and fair, bursting with fruit and grain and flowers. A man and a woman emerged from beneath the roots of the

In the final battle at Ragnarok, the whole world was consumed in fire.

sacred tree Yggdrasil, where they had sheltered while the Earth burned. Nourished on the morning dews, they would people the world, and all would live together in perfect peace and happiness.

At last came a day when Balder rose from the dark underworld. He journeyed to the ruins of Asgard, where he met his brother Hod and four youths who had escaped the devastation. Together the young gods walked the green new grass of heaven, remembering days long past. They thought of Fenrir and the terrible Midgard Serpent. They spoke of Loki and the evil frost giants. But mostly they told wonderful tales of the old gods and goddesses: of Tyr the brave and Frey the good, of Idun's magic apples and Thor's mighty hammer, of Odin, great in wisdom, father of them all.

> IN WONDROUS BEAUTY ONCE AGAIN SHALL THE GOLDEN TABLES STAND MID THE GRASS.
> — *VOLUSPA*, THE *POETIC EDDA*

GLOSSARY

Aesir (AY-zir) the main group of Norse gods, which included Odin and Thor. The Aesir were gods of war and destiny.

archaeologists scientists who study the physical remains of past cultures to learn about human life and activity

Asgard the world of the gods, which floated on a plain far above the world of humans

Bifrost (BIH-frust) rainbow bridge connecting Asgard and Midgard

deity a god, goddess, or other divine being

Germanic peoples a major group of related tribes who lived in Scandinavia and Germany as early as 1000 BCE and spread across much of Europe. The Germanic peoples spoke variations on a language known as Germanic, which developed into English, German, Dutch, and several Scandinavian languages.

immortal living forever

Jotunheim (YO-tun-hime) the land of the giants

legend a traditional story that may involve ordinary mortals as well as divine beings and may be partly based on real people and events

mead a sweet alcoholic beverage made from honey, water, grain, and yeast

Above:
The original Germanic alphabet was made up of twenty-four runes.

Midgard the world of human beings

Mjollnir (muh-YUL-nir) the magic war hammer of Thor. *Mjollnir* means "Crusher."

Muspellheim (MOOS-pel-hime) the world of fire, ruled by the fire giant Surt

mythology the whole body of myths belonging to a people

myths traditional stories about gods and other divine beings, which were developed by ancient cultures to explain the mysteries of the physical and spiritual worlds

Niflheim (NIFF-el-hime) the ancient world of the dead

Norns three goddesses who spun a thread of life for every living being, determining its destiny from birth to death

prophecy a foretelling of something that will happen in the future

Ragnarok (RAG-nuh-rahk) the final battle between gods and giants that would bring about the destruction of the world. *Ragnarok* means "Doom of the Gods."

runes letters of an ancient alphabet used by a number of Germanic peoples, including the Vikings

skalds Scandinavian poets who often traveled from court to court, composing verses in honor of the kings and chieftains

Valhalla the golden hall of the god Odin, where the souls of fallen heroes dwelled after death. *Valhalla* means "Hall of the Slain."

Valkyries (val-KIR-eez) mythical warrior maidens who met the souls of brave warriors who died in battle and led them to Valhalla

Vanir (VAH-nir) the second of the two main groups of Norse gods. The Vanir, who included Njord, Frey, and Freyja, were gods of fertility and prosperity.

Yggdrasil (IG-druh-sill) the huge ash tree that bound the nine mythological worlds together; also known as the World Tree

BIOGRAPHICAL DICTIONARY
of NORSE WRITERS

Our list of Norse writers is very short because the names of most of the early Scandinavian poets and storytellers have been forgotten. For centuries Norse poems and stories about the gods were memorized and passed down orally, rather than recorded in books. Many tales were probably lost forever. The two best surviving sources of the Norse myths are Snorri Sturluson's *Prose Edda* and the *Poetic Edda*.

The *Poetic Edda*

A collection of thirty-four poems that were composed at various times between the ninth century and the mid-thirteenth century. The poems were collected and written down in Iceland sometime around the end of the thirteenth century. Our book includes references to four poems from the *Poetic Edda: Voluspa,* or "The Wise-Woman's Prophecy"; *Hávamál,* or "The Speech of the High One"; *För Skírnis,* or "Skirnir's Journey"; and *Lokasenna,* or "Loki's Wrangling."

Snorri Sturluson
around 1179-1241

Snorri Sturluson was an Icelandic political leader, historian, and poet. His writings are one of our most important sources of information on Norse mythology. His best-known works include *Heimskringla,* a collection of sagas on the lives of Norway's kings, and the *Prose Edda*. The *Prose Edda* contains Snorri's retellings of mythological tales as well as excerpts from traditional Scandinavian poetry.

An early manuscript of
Snorri Sturluson's *Prose Edda*

Thjódólf of Hvin
around 860-935

The Norwegian poet Thjódólf of Hvin served as one of the skalds, or court poets, of King Harald Fairhair of Norway. Only two of his poems have survived: *Haustlöng* ("Autumn-Long") is a "shield poem," written in praise of the mythological scenes depicted on a battle shield. *Ynglingatal* ("The Tally of the Ynglings") blends fact and legends to celebrate the lives of King Harald's ancestors.

The LIVING MYTHS

The Viking Age ended a thousand years ago, but Norse mythology has lived on. The tales of the early Scandinavians have influenced the work of writers, filmmakers, artists, and other creative people all around the world. Here are just a few of the many areas in which the myths of the Norsemen have touched our modern world.

Language

English words derived from Norse mythology include several days of the week: *Tuesday* ("Tyr's Day"), *Wednesday* ("Woden's [Odin's] Day"), *Thursday* ("Thor's Day"), and *Friday* ("Frigg's Day").

Literature

The Hobbit and *The Lord of the Rings* (J. R. R. Tolkien); *The Chronicles of Narnia* (C. S. Lewis); *The Weirdstone of Brisingamen* (Alan Garner); *Legends of Lone Wolf* series (Joe Dever and John Grant); *Wodan's Children* series (Diana Paxson); *Dragonlance Chronicles Trilogy* (Margaret Weis and Tracy Hickman); *Forgotten Realms: Icewind Dale Trilogy* (R. A. Salvatore); *The Wheel of Time* series (Robert Jordan).

Movies and TV

Movies: *The Mask* (1994); *The Lord of the Rings: The Fellowship of the Ring* (2001), *The Two Towers* (2002), and *The Return of the King* (2003); *Chronicles of Narnia: The Lion, the Witch, and the Wardrobe* (2005).
Anime series: *Mythical Detective Loki Ragnarok.*

Music

The Ring of the Nibelung (opera cycle, Richard Wagner).

To FIND OUT MORE

BOOKS

Auerbach, Loren, and Jacqueline Simpson. *Sagas of the Norsemen: Viking and German Myth.* London: Duncan Baird Publishers, 1997.

Branston, Brian. *Gods and Heroes from Viking Mythology.* New York: Peter Bedrick Books, 1994.

Colum, Padraic. *The Children of Odin: The Book of Northern Myths.* New York: Aladdin, 2004.

Daly, Kathleen N. *Norse Mythology A to Z: A Young Reader's Companion.* Revised by Marian Rengel. New York: Facts on File, 2003.

D'Aulaire, Ingri, and Edgar Parin D'Aulaire. *D'Aulaires' Book of Norse Myths.* New York: New York Review of Books, 2005.

Hamilton, Edith. *Mythology: Timeless Tales of Gods and Heroes.* New York: Warner Books, 1999.

Hinds, Kathryn. *The Vikings.* New York: Benchmark Books, 1998.

Osborne, Mary Pope. *Favorite Norse Myths.* New York: Scholastic, 1996.

Philip, Neil. *Odin's Family: Myths of the Vikings.* New York: Orchard Books, 1996.

Schomp, Virginia. *The Vikings.* New York: Scholastic, 2005.

WEB SITES

Encyclopedia Mythica at http://www.pantheon.org
   This online encyclopedia contains more than seven thousand entries on the myths, folktales, and legends of many different cultures. Click on "Norse Mythology" for nearly 150 articles on the gods, monsters, heroes, worlds, and sources of the ancient Scandinavian myths.

Germanic Myths, Legends, and Sagas at
   http://www.pitt.edu/~dash/mythlinks.html
   D. L. Ashliman, a folklore researcher and retired professor of German, compiled this helpful collection of links to sites on Germanic geography, culture, mythology, monuments, and electronic texts.

History for Kids: Ancient German Religion at
   http://www.historyforkids.org/learn/germans/religion/index.htm

Explore the myths and religion of the ancient Germanic peoples, who included the Norsemen. Prepared by Dr. Karen Carr, Associate Professor of History at Portland State University, this easy-to-read site includes links to information on Thor, Freyja, Loki, and other Norse mythological beings.

The Online Medieval & Classical Library: The Story of the Volsungs at http://omacl.org/Volsunga

The Story of the Volsungs is one of the most exciting Norse legendary tales, recounting the adventures of the mighty hero Sigurd and the Valkyrie Brynhild. This electronic edition is based on the translation by William Morris and Eirikr Magnusson. The site also includes excerpts from the *Poetic Edda.*

The Prose Edda at http://www.sacred-texts.com/neu/pre

Snorri Sturluson's *Prose Edda* is one of our most important sources of information on the Norse gods and their adventures. This electronic edition is based on the translation by Arthur Gilchrist Brodeur.

Windows to the Universe: Norse Mythology at http://www.windows.ucar.edu/tour/link=/mythology/norse_culture.html Presented by the University of Michigan, this award-winning site helps students and teachers explore the connections between Earth and space sciences and the Norse myths. The text is offered in three reading levels, for elementary, middle school, and high school students.

SELECTED BIBLIOGRAPHY

Bellows, Henry Adams, trans. *The Poetic Edda.* New York: American-Scandinavian Foundation, 1968.

Bulfinch, Thomas. *The Golden Age of Myth and Legend.* Hertfordshire, England: Wordsworth Reference, 1993.

Cotterell, Arthur. *Norse Mythology.* New York: Smithmark Publishers, 1997.

Crossley-Holland, Kevin. *The Norse Myths.* New York: Pantheon, 1980.

Davidson, H. R. Ellis. *Gods and Myths of the Viking Age.* New York: Barnes and Noble Books, 1996.

Grant, John. *An Introduction to Viking Mythology.* Secaucus, NJ:
    Chartwell Books, 2002.

Guerber, H. A. *Myths of the Norsemen: From the Eddas and Sagas.* New
    York: Dover, 1992.

Haywood, John. *Encyclopaedia of the Viking Age.* New York: Thames &
    Hudson, 2000.

Lindow, John. *Norse Mythology: A Guide to the Gods, Heroes, Rituals, and
    Beliefs.* New York: Oxford University Press, 2001.

Murray, Alexander S. *Manual of Mythology.* Edited by William H.
    Klapp. New York: Tudor, 1935.

Orchard, Andy. *Cassell Dictionary of Norse Myth and Legend.* London:
    Cassell, 1997.

Page, R. I. *Norse Myths.* Austin: University of Texas Press, 1993.

Sturluson, Snorri. *The Prose Edda.* Translated by Jean I. Young.
    Berkeley: University of California Press, 1964.

NOTES *on* QUOTATIONS

Quoted passages in sidebars come from the following sources:

"How the Sun and Moon Cross the Sky," page 39; "Loki the Trickster,"
    page 47; and "The Dwarfs Work Their Magic," page 69, from Snorri
    Sturluson, *The Prose Edda,* translated by Jean I. Young (Berkeley:
    University of California Press, 1964).

"Odin's Quest for Wisdom," page 57, from the *Poetic Edda,* translated by
    Benjamin Thorpe, at http://www.northvegr.org/lore/poetic2/006_07.php

"For the Honor of Thor," page 63, from H. R. Ellis Davidson, *Gods and
    Myths of the Viking Age* (New York: Barnes and Noble Books, 1996).

"The Gods Punish Loki," page 85, from *The Poetic Edda,* translated by
    Henry Adams Bellows (New York: American-Scandinavian
    Foundation, 1968).

INDEX

ABOUT THE AUTHOR

"I can't think of a better way to learn about the people of ancient cultures than by reading the stories that held their deepest hopes and fears, their most cherished values and beliefs. While collecting these sacred tales, I looked for the elements that set each culture apart: the special music of the language, the differing roles of men and women, the unique ways of interpreting the mysteries of life. I also enjoyed discovering the many feelings and experiences that unite all peoples around the world, both past and present. Pueblo storyteller Harold Littlebird said it best: 'We know we all come from story. They may not all be the same story but there is a sameness. There is a oneness in it all.'"

VIRGINIA SCHOMP has written more than sixty titles for young readers on topics including dolphins, dinosaurs, occupations, American history, and world history. Ms. Schomp earned a Bachelor of Arts degree in English Literature from Penn State University. She lives in the Catskill Mountain region of New York with her husband, Richard, and their son, Chip.